Cambridge
Early Years

Communication and Language

for English as a First Language

Learner's Book 3A

Gill Budgell

Contents

Note to parents and practitioners

This Learner's Book provides activities to support the first term of FLE Communication and Language for Cambridge Early Years 3.

Activities can be used at school or at home. Children will need support from an adult. Additional guidance about activities can be found in the **For practitioners** boxes.

Stories are provided for children to enjoy looking at and listening to. Children are not expected to be able to read the stories themselves.

Children will encounter the following characters within this book. You could ask children to point to the characters when they see them on the pages, and say their names.

The Learner's Book activities support the Teaching Resource activities. The Teaching Resource provides step-by-step coverage of the Cambridge Early Years curriculum and guidance on how the Learner's Book activities develop the curriculum learning statements.

Hi, my name is Mia.

Find us on the front covers doing lots of fun activities.

Hi, my name is Gemi.

Hi, my name is Rafi.

Hi, my name is Kiho.

Bubbles by James Carter

Red bubble
Yellow bubble
Orange bubble blue

Pink bubble
Purple bubble
Rainbow bubble too

This bubble
Big bubble
Shiny and round

Float bubble
Fly bubble
Rise from the ground

Up bubble
Up bubble
Up so high

Go bubble
Go bubble
Gone –
Bye bye!

Bubbles

Listen and colour.

Listen to the poem. Colour in the bubbles to match the colours you hear.

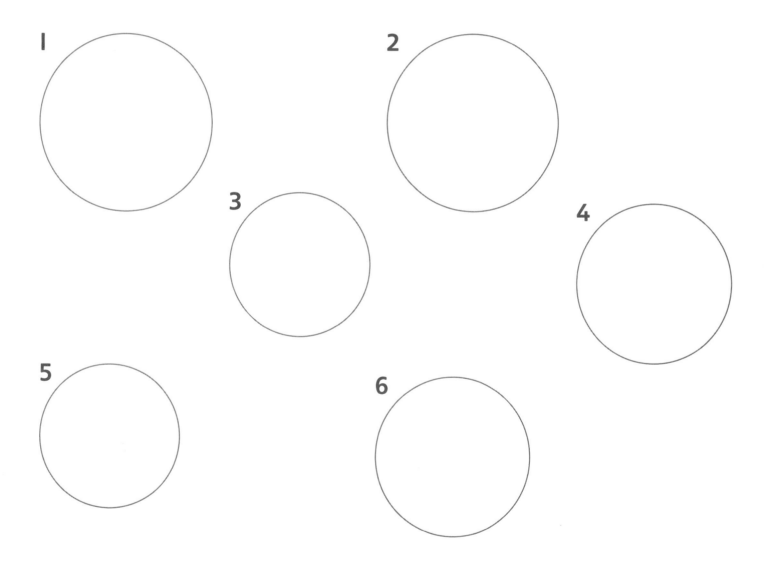

1

2

3

4

5

6

For practitioners

Recite and read the first part of the poem. Tell children they need to listen and colour in the bubbles to match the colours they hear in the poem. e.g., *red, yellow, orange, pink, purple, rainbow*. Some children may wish to draw more bubbles on the page.

Dumpling Day by Meera Sriram

Dumpling party today in town!

Let's all cook and hurry down.

Spicy samosas point to the sky.
Didi is bringing chutney to try.

1 little dumpling on our plate now!

Apple dumplings are doughy and sweet.

Mom serves up a sticky treat.

I dumpling before, then we add I more. How many dumplings now? 2!

Stuffed wu-gok is a crunchy nest.

Gor gor always fries them best.

2 dumplings before, then we add I more. How many dumplings now? 3!

Fufu balls are too soft to chew
Auntie will serve a nutty stew.

3 dumplings before,
then we add 1 more.
How many dumplings now? 4!

Crispy gyoza is filled with tasty mix.
Oji-san packs pairs of chopsticks.

4 dumplings before,
then we add 1 more.
How many dumplings now? 5!

Golden bourekas cool on the rack.
Saba samples the puffy pastry snack.

5 dumplings before,
then we add 1 more.
How many dumplings now? 6!

Warm tamales are wrapped in corn husk.
Prima steams them from dawn to dusk.

6 dumplings before,
then we add 1 more.
How many dumplings now? 7!

Shish barak comes with a tangy hint.
Baba garnishes with parsley and mint.

7 dumplings before,
then we add 1 more.
How many dumplings now? 8!

Pelmeni pop out of trays that gleam.
Babushka scoops thick sour cream.

8 dumplings before,
then we add 1 more.
How many dumplings now? 9!

Ravioli burst with soft cheese.

Bambino begs,

"Can I have one, please!"

9 dumplings before,
then we add 1 more.
How many dumplings now? 10!

10 little dumplings
and people to greet,
10 little dumplings
ready to eat.

We eat and laugh and gather round,
We party till the sun goes down.

10, 9, 8, 7, 6, 5, 4, 3, 2

And this last 1 is for you!

The party food

Match.

Match the labels to the party food.

5   gyoza dumplings

10   ravioli dumplings

3   wu-gok dumplings

9   pelmeni dumplings

4   fufu ball dumplings

6   golden boureka dumplings

1   samosa dumpling

7   tamale dumplings

2   apple dumplings

8   shish barak dumplings

I like to eat

Draw and say.

Draw things you like to eat at a party.
Say their names. Describe them. Try to write the words.

I like to eat bugs!

For practitioners

Children talk about and draw things they like to eat at a party. Encourage them to use the adjectives from the book to link new meanings to those they know, e.g., *spicy*, *doughy*, *sweet*, *crunchy*, *soft*. Support those who want to caption their pictures, e.g., *sweet grapes*.

How many dumplings now?

Listen and repeat.

Look at the picture. Listen to the words.
Make your voice sound the same.

I dumpling before,
then we add I more.
How many dumplings now?

Dumpling Day

Play.

Roll the dice.

Move your counter forwards the same number.

If you land on the girl, go back to the start!

If you land on the knife and fork, skip two spaces ahead!

When you get to the flags, you are the winner!

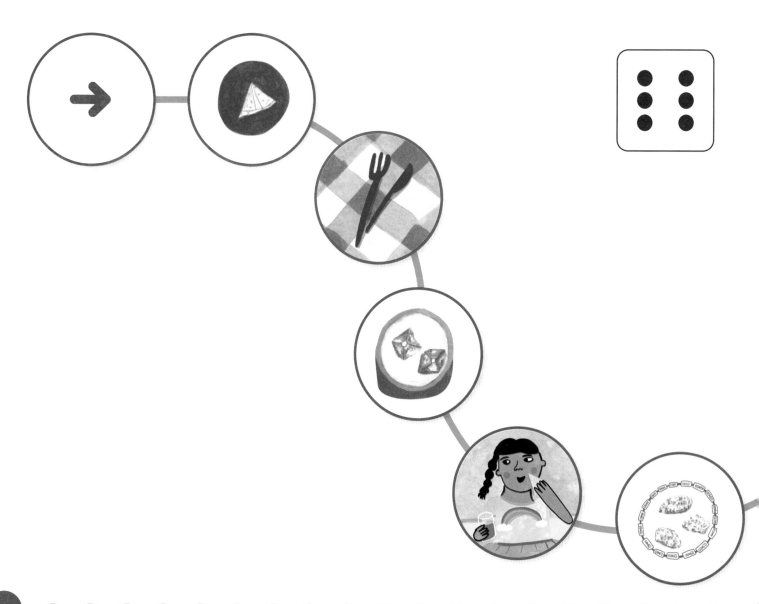

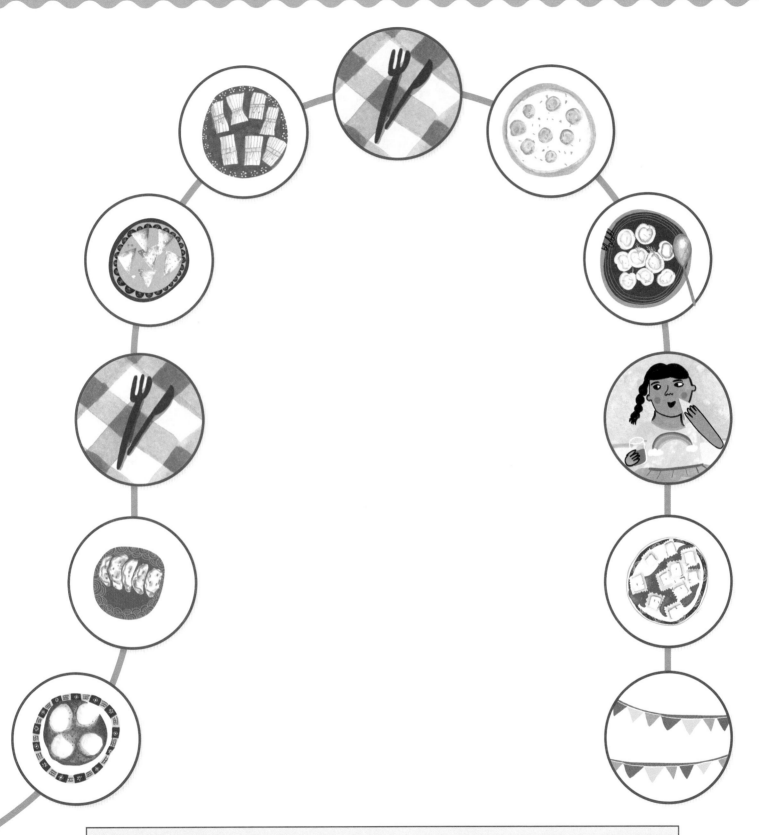

For practitioners

Children play a simple board game to show their understanding of the story and some of the words they have encountered. They will need counters and a six-sided dice (or dot-patterned cards).
The aim is to talk and play. The winner is the first person to get to the flags at the end.

The **Park** in the **Dark**

by Martin Waddell

When the sun goes down and the moon comes
up and the old swing creaks in the dark,
that's when we go to the park,
me and Loopy and Little Gee, all three.

Softly down the staircase, through the haunty
hall, trying to look small,
me and Loopy and Little Gee, we three.

It's shivery out in the dark on our way to the park,
down dustbin alley, past the ruined mill, so still,
just me and Loopy and little Gee, just three.

In the park in the dark by the lake and the bridge,
that's when we see where we want to be,
me and Loopy and Little Gee, WHOOPEE!

And we swing and we slide and we dance and we jump and we chase all over the place,
me and Loopy and Little Gee, the Big Three!

And then the THING comes!

YAAAA AAA!!!

OOOOOEEEEEEE!

RUN RUN RUN shouts Little Gee to Loopy and me and we flee,
me and Loopy and Little Gee, scared three.

Back where we've come through the park in the dark
and the THING is roaring and following, see?
After me and Loopy and Little Gee, we three.

Up to the house, to the stair, to the bed where we ought to be,
me and Loopy and Little Gee, safe as can be, all three.

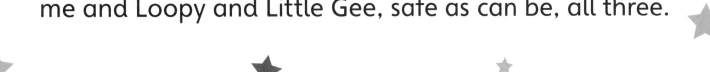

The Park in the Dark sounds

Point and say.

Point to each picture.
Say the sound you think it makes.

a cat 	**a tree blowing in the wind** 	**a dustbin lid hitting the ground** 
an old swing 	**a night train** 	**a police car** 

The THING

Think and draw.

The THING was a train in the rhyme.
Think of a different THING. Draw it.

The THING is _____ .

Doctor Alma and Mr Robot by Rachel Delahaye

Alma was outside, playing Fly High with her favourite toy,
Mr Robot.
"Let's fly even higher!" she said.
She thought Mr Robot looked excited about that,

so Alma swung her arm round
and round and LET GO!

The toy went up and up … higher then
higher … and over the garden wall.
"GO, MR ROBOT!"

Alma found Mr Robot on the other
side of the wall in a muddy puddle.
"You went so high!" said Alma.

But then she noticed Mr Robot's broken arm. "Uh-oh. I think you need to go hospital!"

She thought Mr Robot looked sad about that, so Alma took him inside and put him down on a towel.

"Don't be sad, hospital is where you go to get better. I'll be your doctor."

Doctor Alma wet a sponge and told Mr Robot about the time she fell off her bike.

"When I went to hospital, the doctor cleaned the cut on my knee to stop germs getting in."

She thought Mr Robot looked worried about that, so she dabbed the sponge as gently as she could.

"Don't be worried, this won't hurt. There … all clean," she said.

Now, the tricky bit.
Alma remembered how the doctor who looked at her knee told funny jokes to take her mind off the pain.

"What's a robot's favourite game?
Not Hide and Seek but … Hide and Beep!"

She thought Mr Robot looked pleased at that, so she told a few more jokes as she examined the broken arm.

Soon Alma was laughing, and Mr Robot was jiggling and all the pain was forgotten.

Hmmm, the doctor gave me stitches, but I think you need glue," she said. Alma dabbed the break with a glue stick and pushed Mr Robot's arm back in place.

"Now I'm going to put a plaster on your arm to hold it together while the glue dries."

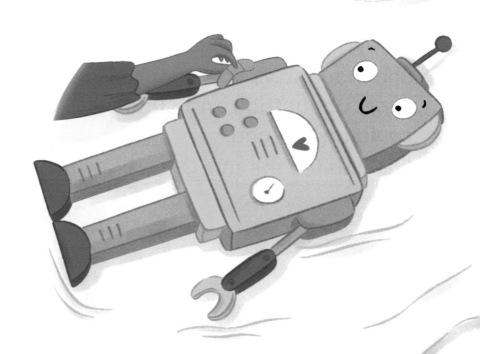

She thought Mr Robot looked nervous about that, so Alma decided to give her toy a boost.

"Don't be nervous. You're SO BRAVE, Mr Robot," she said.

"You're doing so well."

When the glue was dry, the arm looked as good as new, apart from a small crack.

"You're all better! There's just a tiny line," Alma said.
She thought Mr Robot looked upset about that, and Alma could understand.
She had felt the same.

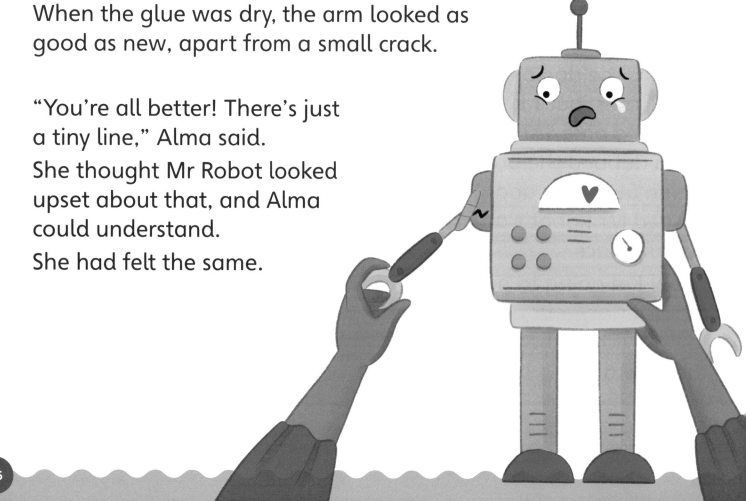

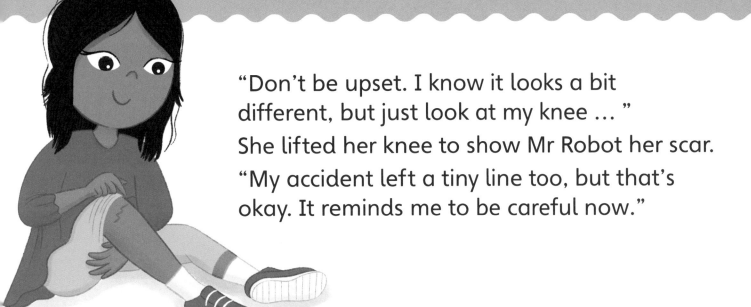

"Don't be upset. I know it looks a bit different, but just look at my knee … "
She lifted her knee to show Mr Robot her scar.
"My accident left a tiny line too, but that's okay. It reminds me to be careful now."

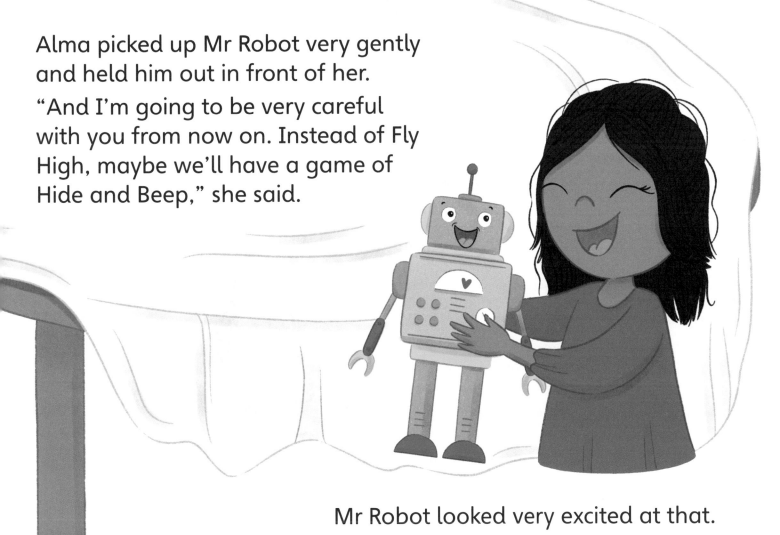

Alma picked up Mr Robot very gently and held him out in front of her.
"And I'm going to be very careful with you from now on. Instead of Fly High, maybe we'll have a game of Hide and Beep," she said.

Mr Robot looked very excited at that.

How is Mr Robot feeling?

Look and say.

Look at each picture of Mr Robot.
Say how Mr Robot is feeling and why.

Oh no! What's wrong?

Mark and say.

Look at each picture. Tick ✔ the things that are not broken. Cross ✗ the things that are broken. Say what is wrong with the broken things.

29

Fix the sentences

Write and say.

Fix each sentence.
Write it with a capital letter and a full stop.

All sentences start with a _____.

alma was playing with her toy

_____

the toy went up and up

_____

the toy broke

_____

alma fixed it

_____

My toy

Show and say.

Paste a photo of a toy. Describe it.
Say why you chose it.

My toy is _____ .

Acknowledgements

The authors and publishers acknowledge the following sources of copyright material and are grateful for the permissions granted.
While every effort has been made, it has not always been possible to identify the sources of all the material used, or to trace all copyright holders.
If any omissions are brought to our notice, we will be happy to include the appropriate acknowledgements on reprinting.

'Bubbles' by James Carter, used with permission of the author.

Dumpling Day Text copyright © 2021 by Meera Sriram. Illustrations copyright © 2021 by Inés de Antuñano. Used with permission from Barefoot Books, Ltd.

THE PARK IN THE DARK Written by Martin Waddell & Illustrated by Barbara Firth. Text © 1989 Martin Waddell. Reproduced by permission of Walker Books Ltd, London, SE11 5HJ www.walker.co.uk

Thanks to the following artists at Beehive Illustration:

Nadene Neude, Claire Philpott.

Cover characters by Becky Davies (The Bright Agency)